To: Erica
May you,
continue to experience the
joy God has planned for you!
Pastor Mouton

Forgiveness

The Turning Point to Good Endings

Larry J. Mouton Jr.

Renown Publishing

Forgiveness / Larry J. Mouton Jr.
ISBN-13: 978-1-945793-94-3

It is with heartfelt gratitude that I
dedicate this book to my loving parents:

My mother, Rena Sam—
Who taught me to love compassionately.

My father, Leo Sam—
Who instructed me to serve courageously!

Also, to my beautiful and brilliant wife, Reba Mouton—
Who has profoundly inspired me to pen my convictions about
our Lord and Savior, Jesus Christ.

And to our children, Hanna and Joshuah Mouton—
Whom God entrusted to our stewardship.

Finally, to my entire No Greater Love Church family—
Whom I am honored and privileged to lead in a
growing and meaningful relationship with our
Lord and Savior, Jesus Christ.

To God be the glory!

CONTENTS

The Gift

Consider the following twist on the story of the prodigal son. A father in Spain went looking for his estranged son, who had run away from home. He searched high and low, but he could not find his son. Finally, the father had the idea to place an ad in a Madrid newspaper: "Son, meet me at noon on Saturday in front of this newspaper office. I forgive you. I love you. Your father."

That Saturday, *eight hundred* sons arrived at the newspaper office—eight hundred sons looking for reconciliation with their fathers![1]

What does this story tell you about the extent of broken, busted relationships in our world? Everywhere you look there are fractured relationships of every variety: between husbands and wives, parents and children, friends, family members, and co-workers. Those individual fractures show up in our society, too—in our communities, workplaces, government, and even our churches.

If you need more evidence, browse the "self-help" section of Amazon or your library or local bookstore. The number of self-help books dealing with relationships is truly vast. This tells us two things: first, we have a lot of ruptured relationships in our culture; and second, there is no shortage of supposed experts who offer answers.

What do we do about all of this brokenness in our lives? Do we put countless ads in the paper and hope that people show up looking for reconciliation? Even if people do want to come together again, what are the tools for reconciliation?

There are many tools in that toolbox—hope, humility, and courage, among others—but one of the indispensable tools is *forgiveness*. Without it, old wounds fester until they become new wounds, and reconciliation is stunted.

We have good intentions, especially at the start of a new relationship, but inevitably something goes amiss. What do we want then? We want what those eight hundred sons wanted: forgiveness, reconciliation, and restoration. All three are not always possible, but forgiveness is something we can control. Whatever has happened, forgiveness is possible. Forgiveness is a prerequisite for a life of freedom. We must exercise forgiveness if we want a full, healthy, and free life. It simply isn't optional.

But it's challenging, isn't it? You've experienced those challenges if you've ever tried extending forgiveness. However, the challenges should not stop us, because the Lord God has given us all the provision we need to use this tool. Forgiveness goes against the grain of our fallen, sinful human nature, but the Lord gives us supernatural power to exercise it. He gives us His Word, He gives us the examples of others, and He gives us His Holy Spirit to help us overcome our tendency to live in unforgiveness. He gives us all we need to walk in freedom, including the power to forgive.

In the following pages, we're going to explore that essential tool of forgiveness. We're going to look at how our relationships are sabotaged by ourselves and by others. We're going to learn what forgiveness is and what it is not. We're going to explore the benefits of forgiveness and how it can lead to beautiful reconciliation and restoration.

Throughout the book, you'll read stories from my life, from the experiences of others, and, most importantly, from the Word of God. The Bible speaks volumes on the topic of forgiveness. With the help of workbook questions, journal prompts, and action steps, we will examine some practical ways to use the tool of forgiveness.

We can live hampered, or we can live free. The choice is ours. God has given us all we need to live free. It's our job to take hold of the gift of forgiveness—the gift He has given us through His Son, Jesus Christ—and employ it in our lives to experience its freedom, power, and beauty.

Let's choose forgiveness. Let's choose freedom.

CHAPTER ONE

Sabotage!

Did you know that federal agents don't learn to spot counterfeit money by studying the counterfeits? They study genuine bills until they master the look and feel of the real thing. Then they recognize bogus money when they see it. In a similar way, a heart surgeon first has to understand the original design and function of a healthy heart for there to be any hope of restoring a damaged one.

The same is true for relationships. In order to understand what healthy relationships look like, we first need to understand God's original design for them. When we're intimately familiar with what healthy relationships look like, we can easily spot one that is unhealthy, and we'll know how to respond.

The Example of the Trinity

Before the foundation of the world, the Trinitarian God existed: Father, Son, and Holy Spirit. The Trinity is the epitome of what relationships were meant to be. In the Trinity, Jesus does not veer from the Holy Spirit, and the Holy Spirit does not behave incongruously with the Father. The members of this mysterious Trinity operate in total harmony, unity, and agreement.

Jesus said repeatedly that He did only as the Father directed (John 5:19–20, 30; John 8:28–29). When the Holy Spirit came, He came at the direction of the Father and in the name of the Son to remind the disciples of Jesus' teaching (John 14:16–18, 26). The Father declared that He was "well pleased" with His Son (Matthew 3:17). New believers are baptized in the name of the Father, the Son, and the Holy Spirit.

When this Trinitarian God created humankind, what did He say? He said, "Let us make mankind in our image…" (Genesis 1:26). Why did He say "our"? Because He is three in one. He is a Trinity.

Modeled After the Trinity

When we were made, it was in the image of this harmonious relationship among the Father, the Son, and the Spirit. Being made in the Trinity's image means that we have the capacity for the same kind of relationship that exists within the Trinity.

Like God, we have the capacity for moral awareness, intelligence, creativity, emotions, and relationships. Like Him, we were made for harmony, unity, and agreement with one another. That's why Jesus said that the greatest commandments are to love the Lord our God with all of our being and to love one another as we love ourselves

(Matthew 22:37–39).

Furthermore, just as the members of the Trinity are interdependent, we were made to complement and need one another. In Genesis 2, the Lord declared that it was "not good for the man to be alone," and He made a woman as his complement (Genesis 2:18–24). Our original design, before the fall from the Garden of Eden, had us in relationship with one another—needing, giving, and receiving.

We live in a world where self-sufficiency and independence are gods, but that's not the world we were made for! God made us for one another. Jesus, even while fully human and fully divine, longed for His original unity with the Father and the Spirit while He was on earth (John 17:5). To this day, even the creation longs for the restoration of this unity (Romans 8:19–23).

In short, we are modeled after the Trinity in our potential and in our purpose. We were created to be like God. We were not created to *be* God, but to be *like* Him in unified relationship. As Psalm 133:1 says, "How good and pleasant it is when God's people live together in unity!"

What Went Wrong?

It seems that something has gone awry. Why else would those eight hundred sons answer a newspaper ad offering reconciliation with a father? What makes relationships so challenging?

One answer is that we're simply different from each other. Our differences actually have the potential to make our relationships more beautiful. I have weaknesses and strengths, just as you have weaknesses and strengths. Together, we can complement and supplement one another like a well-functioning athletic team. But as you know, this is not how it often works in real life. Our differences easily become stumbling blocks. I say "y'all," you say "you guys," and some people say "you'ns." One church has elders, one has deacons, and one has a board—and that's just in the Baptist denomination! Rather than accepting these superficial differences, we often use them to separate and categorize one another. Honestly, there's no limit to the ways we allow, and sometimes even encourage, our differences to divide us. We are complex, and our complexities can drive wedges between us.

Communication is another culprit behind the difficulty of relationships. We don't always communicate clearly. We operate on assumptions, past hurts that haven't been addressed, resentments, and unexpressed or poorly expressed expectations. We must talk with one another calmly, consistently, and clearly if we want to experience unity in our relationships.

The Fourth Player

Social scientists say that our relationships are made up of a vast, dynamic network of influencers and contributors. They identify three players in this network: God, others, and ourselves. But they forget the fourth dynamic: Satan. And that's fine with him. Our accuser wishes to remain anonymous and faceless, because his potential damage is greatest when he's allowed to operate behind the scenes. The apostle Paul told us to "put on the full armor of God" (Ephesians 6:10–18) so we would be prepared to stand against the devil's onslaughts. Our enemy, and God's, wants to diminish our capacity to bring God glory and live in His image as He designed us to do. Peter wrote, "Be alert and of sober mind. Your enemy the devil prowls around like a roaring lion looking for someone to devour" (1 Peter 5:8). Jesus said, "The thief comes only to steal and kill and destroy; I have come that they may have life, and have it to the full" (John 10:10). We need to realize that this fourth player, Satan, is active and on the prowl. The enemy has several tricks to sabotage our relationships, including deception, resignation, passiveness, and shame. We need to be aware of and understand each one.

Deception

Satan deceives by his very nature (John 8:44). He will persuade you to accept something as true and valid when it simply isn't. He will tell you, "They meant to hurt you," whether they did or not. He will tell you, "She's never believed in you," even if you have years of evidence that she has. He will tell you, "God has never looked out for you," even though your Christian friends are right there pointing out the dozens of ways God has taken care of you just in the last year.

If you listen to the devil long enough, he'll have you questioning God's foundational love and care for you in every way he can. He will use any ploy in his toolbox—every slight, every hurt, every disappointment—to convince you that God isn't looking out for you.

Resignation, Passiveness, and Shame

Whenever you engage in dialogue with the enemy, you find yourself resigning from the truth you once knew and from standing by your convictions, just as Eve did with the Tree of Knowledge of Good and Evil. You stop fighting, stop believing, and stop trusting. You may hear these types of statements in your head:

"This relationship just isn't worth it anymore."

"I can't keep trying."

"They just don't care, so I won't care, either."

"God doesn't care about my happiness and my relationships."

These emotions lead to isolation, loneliness, and further brokenness. There's a saying that the devil gets you both coming and going with the sin and the shame associated with it.

When we feel shame, we often blame other people. When God came looking for Adam "in the garden in the cool of the day," Adam emerged from his hiding and blamed Eve (Genesis 3:8–12). Eve turned around and blamed the serpent (Genesis 3:13). Their shame led them to blame—blaming others, that is.

When we feel shame, we also tend to become passive. We simply sit and let the brokenness sink deeper and deeper into our souls. We don't believe that it was our fault, so we don't pursue the repair.

Back to the Drawing Board

Remember that God made us to walk together in harmony, as He does with the Son and the Holy Spirit. There may be differences between us, and sometimes it's difficult to communicate, but we need to spend enough time talking and praying together to pursue reconciliation.

The Bible tells us, "Resist the devil, and he will flee from you" (James 4:7). We resist his deception and his push toward resignation, passiveness, and shame when we rely on God's truth and refuse to yield to the devil's temptation. We can stand against Satan when we stand on God's Word!

One of the greatest tools we have against our enemy is forgiveness. When we forgive, we break chains. When we forgive, we pursue unity. When we forgive, we find freedom. The devil can't stand it when we practice forgiveness. It's a slap in the face to him. More importantly, it's a sign of our living free, whole, and unified in the image of God.

However, we first need to understand what exactly forgiveness is. I believe that this understanding begins with knowing the forgiveness of sins that comes from the Lord and the sacrifice of Jesus on the cross. The next chapter will delve a little further into what forgiveness is using biblical examples and instruction.

WORKBOOK

Chapter One Questions

Question: Which relationships in your life do you sense are far from the way God intended for them to be? Where is there disunity and divisiveness in your relationships? Are there cultural or personality differences that you have allowed to come between you and others? What communication struggles are making your relationships difficult?

_____

_____

_____

_____

_____

_____

_____

_____

Question: Describe a time when you blamed someone else in order to try to offset your feelings of shame and guilt. How did your attitude of blaming affect that relationship?

_____

_____

_____

_____

_____

_____

_____

_____

_____

_____

Journal: Before reading the next chapter, write down your definition of forgiveness. You will use this in the next chapter to evaluate how well you understand the true nature of what forgiveness is and isn't.

_____

_____

_____

_____

_____

_____

_____

_____

_____

_____

_____

Action: Write down relationships and situations in your life in which forgiveness is needed. Ask God to speak to you as you continue to read through this book and to help you fulfill His design for each of these relationships.

Chapter One Notes

_____

_____

_____

_____

_____

_____

_____

_____

_____

_____

_____

_____

_____

_____

_____

_____

_____

_____

_____

_____

_____

_____

.

CHAPTER TWO

Forgiveness:
What It Is and What It Isn't

The story is told of a pastor asking his congregation, "Who here has learned how to forgive their enemies?"

About half of the congregation half-heartedly lifts a hand. The pastor rephrases his question: "Who here would like to learn how to forgive their enemies?"

Every hand slowly raises, except that of little old Mrs. Sadie in the back. The pastor is surprised.

"Mrs. Sadie, do you not wish to forgive your enemies?"

Mrs. Sadie replies sweetly, "I don't have any enemies, Preacher."

Taken aback, the pastor responds, "Is that right? That is most impressive, Mrs. Sadie! How old are you?"

"I'm ninety-eight, Preacher."

"Mrs. Sadie, would you mind telling the congregation how, at ninety-eight years old, you have managed to have a life free of enemies?"

Mrs. Sadie slowly stands, pauses, and then says, "I've outlived all those jerks."

Needless to say, that isn't forgiveness!

Let's be honest; forgiveness is hard. People will harm you, betray you, treat you unfairly, and disappoint you. Sometimes we're offended on behalf of someone else. You may be angry at an in-law for the abuse of your spouse, an insurance agent for taking advantage of your grandparents, or a teacher for mistreating a child. Sometimes we're offended on behalf of groups, such as when we're offended that children in our community go hungry or factory workers in other countries are abused at work.

The truth is that forgiving others, whether they have offended us directly or indirectly, is no easy task. It requires humility and swallowing our pride, as well as letting go of the stronghold the offender has on us. Oftentimes, we're the ones who need to be forgiven. I'm not sinless, nor are you. We are inherently flawed. The truth is that we all are sinners saved by God's grace, and the only good in us is from Him. Perhaps this is something we should remember when we're tempted to think that we're above needing someone else's forgiveness.

God has instructed each of us to forgive. Jesus exhorted His followers to forgive (Matthew 6:14–15; Mark 11:25; Luke 6: 27–31; John 20:23). Colossians 3:13 takes up the refrain: "Bear with each other and forgive one another if any of you has a grievance against someone. Forgive as the Lord forgave you."

Martin Luther King, Jr., elaborated on this scriptural principle by saying, "We must develop and maintain the capacity to forgive, for he who is devoid of the power to forgive is devoid of the power to love."[2]

If we are to exercise forgiveness, the first thing we need to get straight is what forgiveness is and what it isn't.

Forgiveness Is...

Forgiveness is about the offended more than the offender. The offender, in essence, has power over the offended to bind his or her thoughts and emotions and hold on tight. Forgiveness is about you healing and being delivered from what enslaves you.

A Journey

Life is a journey, and forgiveness is a stop on that journey. Sometimes the journey can be a long one to get to the other side of the path. Like any journey, patience and careful consideration is necessary. You need to take time for it to be real, not contrived, shallow, or forced.

Difficult

Sure, it's easy enough to forget the driver who cut you off, the girl who turned you down for a date (so you eventually met your wife!), or the co-worker who ate the last doughnut in the break room.

But usually forgiveness is more difficult than overlooking minor offenses. Any time we obey the Lord's commands, it won't be easy, but God takes us through it. He gives us strength. He gives us the example of our Savior, His Son. God gives us all the supernatural power we need to forgive.

Corrie ten Boom, who suffered in a concentration camp, was able, years later, to forgive one of the guards at that camp.[3] The Bible tells us that Joseph forgave his scheming brothers for selling him into slavery (Genesis 45:1–15, 50:15–21). Jesus, our perfect example of what it means to be human, forgave His crucifiers (Luke 23:34). If forgiveness for all of these terrible offenses is possible, then we know that God can help you and me to forgive, too.

Christlike

Plain and simple, forgiving others is being like Jesus. God's grace to us is unmerited favor. When we forgive, we are extending unmerited favor to another human being. God's mercy to us is the withholding of deserved punishment. When we forgive, we are withholding all of the available punishment we could give to another. Forgiveness puts us in the company of Jesus and all of the saintly cloud of witnesses who followed Him ahead of us.

How do you exercise Christlike forgiveness? *Renounce your right to hurt back.* Vengeance belongs to the Lord (Romans 12:19). Revenge is a trademark of sin; forgiveness is a trademark of grace.

Stop defining your offenders by their offenses. Recognize your offender as a whole person, not just by what he or she did that hurt you. If God were to define us exclusively by our sins, where would we be? He knows our every sin and loves us anyway. When He looks at us, He sees the precious creation He sent His Son to save. When we can see our offenders as whole people, rather than as offenders, we begin to see them more as the Lord sees them.

Recognize that every offender has an accomplice. Perhaps you've heard the saying that "hurt people hurt people." Maybe she said those hurtful things because the same had been told to her throughout her whole life. Maybe he betrayed you because life has taught him to strike first before he is betrayed. When you remember that your offenders are coming from a place of hurt, it gives you room to forgive them.

Also, remember that our enemy, Satan, is an active player in all of this. Satan is ruthless and purposeful, and he is a major villain in our stories.

God wants you to be set free, and as long as you're walking in unforgiveness—or faking forgiveness—you'll be hampered. Know the difference and seek the true, freeing forgiveness that Jesus modeled for us. Don't try to forget the offense, deny it, minimize it, or pursue an unattainable reconciliation or restoration. Instead, pursue the difficult, but Christlike, process of genuine forgiveness.

You'll reap so many benefits, which is what we will explore in the next chapter.

Forgiveness Isn't…

Some things pass themselves off as forgiveness when, in reality, they are very damaging. We need to recognize the imposters of forgiveness. Sometimes we put on an outward show for people around us in an effort to appear that we have forgiven, yet our souls are still seething with the pain of unforgiveness. Let's unpack what these imposters are and how to deal with them.

Tolerance

Tolerance requires putting up with a person or situation, even if we disagree or disapprove, for the sake of getting along and keeping the peace. Not everybody thinks alike. Not everybody has the same opinions. Not everybody behaves as we'd prefer. That's okay. If everybody were like me, it would be a boring world. It would be just as boring if everybody were like you. In general, an attitude of tolerance allows space for the beauty of our differences to exist.

However, there are limits to what you should tolerate. Tolerating abuse or repeated harassment or brushing aside obnoxious, harmful, or dangerous behaviors will only breed frustration, internal resentment, and an unforgiving spirit.

Forgetting

"Forgive and forget" is one of the most misleading concepts we commonly hear about forgiveness. If you associate forgiveness with any form of amnesia, you will suffer. Eventually you will discredit the very notion of forgiveness altogether.

You cannot forget what happened. This isn't a sci-fi or fantasy movie in which somebody can shine a bright light or wave a wand and cause selective memory loss. Forgiveness does not mean forgetting, but it does mean releasing any bitterness associated with the memory.

Denial of Hurt

Just as forgiveness doesn't mean you forget, it also doesn't mean you should deny that the injury took place. Don't deny the offense, the hurt, or the effect any of it had on you. Recognize and be aware of the traumatic experience that occurred in your life, but also understand your need to forgive.

Forgiveness will never say, "It's no big deal." If the offense weren't a big deal, forgiveness wouldn't be needed. Forgiveness is always honest. It says, "You hurt me. I remember it. It was wrong, but I forgive you anyway."

Restoration or Reconciliation

Restoration and reconciliation are the ultimate goals of forgiveness, but there is no guarantee of either. Forgiveness is a gift you give to the offender, whether or not the offender is deserving, and it is a gift to yourself. Forgiveness can be unilateral, but reconciliation and restoration are two-way streets.

You can forgive an abuser, but it would be unwise to return to that situation. You can forgive an unkindness, but if the offensive party is completely out of your life—maybe even has died—it's not possible to be restored or reconciled. (We will discuss this more in Chapter Six.)

Don't let these imposters pose as elements of forgiveness. They are not the real deal. Don't be fooled. Only genuine, Christlike forgiveness will bring you freedom.

WORKBOOK

Chapter Two Questions

Question: Describe a time when you needed and received forgiveness. How did it impact you, and how can that experience help you in understanding the need to forgive those who have wronged you?

_____

_____

_____

_____

_____

_____

_____

_____

_____

_____

Question: Are you easily offended, or have you developed tolerance toward differing viewpoints? Would you be able to exercise tolerance in each of the following discussions? If not, how can you work on becoming less easily offended and more gracious toward others? Consider discussing:

- Current events with someone who favors a different political party.

- Childrearing with someone who does not parent the way you think is right.

- Health with someone who has an entirely different type of diet from yours.

- Music and entertainment with someone who has different opinions about what is good.

How can a lack of tolerance in a relationship lead to a need for forgiveness?

_____

_____

_____

_____

_____

_____

_____

_____

_____

_____

Journal: How do expectations about forgiveness, such as forgetting the offense or no longer feeling the hurt of the offense, hinder forgiveness? How does accepting the fact that forgiveness is a difficult process help in choosing to forgive? Look back at the definition of forgiveness you wrote in Chapter One and see if you had any unrealistic expectations or misconceptions about forgiveness that you need to correct. Rewrite your definition based on what you know now.

_____

_____

_____

_____

_____

_____

_____

_____

_____

_____

Action: Create a chart contrasting what forgiveness is and what it is not. Add to the list as you think of other items and as you learn more through this book.

Chapter Two Notes

CHAPTER THREE

The Benefits Package

Have you ever gotten one of those jobs with benefits attached? You sit down with a description of the benefits package and read it carefully, looking for medical insurance, dental and vision insurance, a 401(k) option or a pension, vacation and/or paid time off, professional development opportunities, maybe even an offer to help with your education. As you read, maybe you give the package the side-eye because it's not that great, or maybe you're thanking the Lord because it's a good package.

You know that they aren't handing out benefits packages to freeloaders. You know that you're going to have to do some work you don't like, because even a dream job has those aspects and those days. You know that you're going to have to practice a little give and take with other co-workers. But it's okay because there's a salary and there are benefits.

Forgiveness is the same way. It involves work, some of it hard and unpleasant. It involves interaction with others. But it's worth it. It has benefits you can't get from any other pursuit. Should we forgive others just because it's the right thing to do? Sure, but God is an understanding and generous Father, and He offers many payoffs for this difficult task, raising its value and lowering our resistance to it.

Forgiveness Matters

[Withholding forgiveness is like] drinking rat poison and expecting the rat to die.[4]

—Anne Lamott

Forgiveness and unforgiveness both have natural consequences and effects. Forgiveness releases you from bondage and provides freedom, while unforgiveness holds you captive, with detrimental repercussions.

When someone has committed an offense against you and you withhold forgiveness, unforgiveness holds you prisoner. Every time you talk about or dwell on the issue, you reinforce your captivity. In his book *Wishful Thinking*, theologian Frederick Buechner likens an unforgiving attitude to "lick[ing] your wounds," "smacking your lips over grievances long past," "rolling over your tongue the bitter confrontation of those things to come and to savor to the last toothsome morsel the very pain that we are given and the pain that we are giving back." He describes this as a feast fit for a king, with us wolfing down ourselves. The skeleton at the table is you.[5]

Unforgiveness acts as a roadblock, impeding our

progress emotionally, relationally, and spiritually. Jesus said, "And when you stand praying, if you hold anything against anyone, forgive them, so that your Father in heaven may forgive you your sins" (Mark 11:25). There are spiritual consequences to our refusal to forgive other people. It may also inhibit our progress in some material way, such as a job promotion, our finances, or our physical health.

Just like that colorful Monopoly money, unforgiveness won't result in anything of true value. Holding grudges against those who have wronged us isn't going to buy us anything in the game of life. In contrast, think about what we gain when we "overcome evil with good," as Paul instructed us in Romans 12:21. The previous verse shows us how to do just that: "If your enemy is hungry, feed him; if he is thirsty, give him something to drink" (Romans 12:20). Exhibit the love of God to your enemies. It can have life-long, life-changing implications even beyond what you see.

Unforgiveness is a cancer. It causes an internal bitterness that destroys us from the inside out, hardening our hearts and diminishing our capacity for joy. In Ephesians 4:31–32, we see a picture of contrasting behaviors: "Get rid of all bitterness, rage and anger, brawling and slander, along with every form of malice. Be kind and compassionate to one another, forgiving each other, just as in Christ God forgave you." Which of these attitudes do you want to be characterized by? Which leads to a more joyful life?

I'm not saying that we should be gullible. We should glean wisdom from every unfortunate event in our lives and take steps not to go down those paths again. However, we shouldn't allow those experiences to stop us from living. Galatians 5:1 tells us that God has given us liberty. When we forgive, we stand in the liberty Christ Himself gained on our behalf.

There are times when we allow ourselves to hold hard feelings in our hearts because we don't realize that forgiveness will benefit us. We resist forgiveness because we mistakenly think that it:

- Will cost us more than it will benefit us.

- Will result in our offenders winning and us losing.

- Means that we trust again. It doesn't. Forgiveness is a gift; trust is earned.

- Indicates that we forget, minimize, or deny the offense. (See Chapter Two for more on imposters of forgiveness.)

Forgiveness matters to God. The Bible tells us that "while we were still sinners, Christ died for us" (Romans 5:8). The Father went to the furthest lengths possible to offer us forgiveness. He sent His only Son to live, to die, and to rise again so that we could be reconciled to Him.

The Bible tells us to love, to demonstrate grace (unmerited favor), and to forgive each other as God forgave us (Colossians 3:12–14). Jesus modeled the ultimate forgiveness, and we are to model ourselves after Him. As we do, we receive benefits—better than any insurance, retirement, or vacation package anybody could offer!

The Example of Joseph

For a biblical example of forgiveness, let's look at the life of Joseph, whose story we find in Genesis 37 through 50.

Whom did Joseph need to forgive? Well, that's a long list. We could start with his father, Jacob, who made no secret of the fact that Joseph was his favorite of his twelve sons. Jacob gave him a coat of many colors—a showpiece garment, not the hand-me-down jeans all of the other brothers wore to work. Worse, Jacob sent Joseph out to report on his brothers. Talk about stoking sibling rivalry! Naturally, Joseph's brothers were offended by the way their father played favorites (Genesis 37:2–11).

From Joseph's point of view, his first real offenders were his brothers, who sold him into slavery (Genesis 37:18–28). Then there were Mr. and Mrs. Potiphar. When Joseph turned down the sexual advances of his master's wife, she falsely accused him of attempted rape, resulting in Joseph being thrown into an Egyptian prison as an innocent man (Genesis 39).

There was also Joseph's temporary cellmate, Pharaoh's cupbearer. Joseph correctly interpreted the cupbearer's dream that he would be restored to Pharaoh's favor, but when the cupbearer returned to court, he forgot all about mentioning the Hebrew prisoner who had been so helpful to him (Genesis 40).

Joseph was harmed by many people, yet when he came to power and had the opportunity for picture-perfect revenge, he refrained:

> *His brothers then came and threw themselves down before*
> *him. "We are your slaves," they said.*
>
> *But Joseph said to them, "Don't be afraid. Am I in the place*
> *of God? You intended to harm me, but God intended it for*
> *good to accomplish what is now being done, the saving of*
> *many lives. So then, don't be afraid. I will provide for you*
> *and your children." And he reassured them and spoke*
> *kindly to them.*
>
> **—Genesis 50:18–21**

Read those last words again. Joseph was kind to his brothers. He reassured them in their distress. Joseph epitomized godly forgiveness. He had every right to be upset and bitter, but instead he kept his eyes on the prize. He kept his eyes on God. Like Jesus, he endured his pain and shame "for the joy set before him" (Hebrews 12:2). When he was faced with the choice between sweet revenge and difficult forgiveness, he chose the way of his gracious and merciful God, and he reaped the benefits.

The Benefits of Forgiveness

One of the hardest things about forgiveness is releasing our right to demand justice when we've been wronged. It is easy to feel that we're the ones who end up losing when we forgive those who have harmed us. But when our focus is on our loss, we lose sight of what we gain in forgiving others. There are many benefits we receive when we choose the path of forgiveness.

Benefit 1: We become more like Jesus. When Jesus hung on the cross, dying, He said of His crucifiers, "Father, forgive them, for they do not know what they are doing" (Luke 23:34). When we choose to forgive those who have wronged us, we become more like Christ. We also become more like the Father, who gave His only Son (John 3:16). Our Heavenly Father has a lot of experience with defiant and rebellious children—us! When we mimic our Savior and extend forgiveness through the power of the Holy Spirit, we are also behaving like the Father, which pleases Him.

Benefit 2: We experience freedom. Unforgiveness is bondage; forgiveness is freedom. When we forgive, we are no longer carrying the weight of angry or bitter thoughts about our offenders. Whatever they did to us is no longer a chain around our ankles. We may still have wounds to process, and that might take a long time, but we will be released from the exhausting burden of our grudge.

Benefit 3: With freedom comes potential for healing. We will not find healing if we allow wrongdoings to consume our thoughts. Just like malignant cancer has to be removed before the body can be healed, unforgiveness also has to be removed. Just like a broken bone needs to be pointed in the right direction before it can heal correctly, we need to point our hearts toward forgiveness. Healing brings a release that enables us to breathe again and start healing.

Benefit 4: We offer freedom to the offenders. Now, before you get a burr under your saddle and tell me how horrible and undeserving of freedom the offender is, let me remind you of Romans 5:8: "While we were still sinners, Christ died for us."

Let me also remind you of something we discussed back in Chapter Two: every offender has a backstory. Maybe he treated you that way because he was treated that way. Maybe she talked badly about you because people have talked unkindly about her for years. When you forgive, you open the door for your offenders to walk free—not free from consequence or free to mistreat you again, but free to walk away from their sins.

We need to offer others the mercy and grace our Father has so freely offered us. Now, your offenders don't have to receive the forgiveness you extend, and your offering doesn't mean that you trust them again and want to schedule weekly lunch dates. You simply offer the gift of forgiveness; that is all.

Benefit 5: You open the door for reconciliation. When you forgive, you are walking toward reconciliation, or reestablishing a functional relationship at a basic level. Your offender may or may not meet you on that street, but your forgiveness makes the meeting a possibility.

God is in the business of reconciliation. Even before Adam's and Eve's footprints had disappeared from the Garden of Eden, God had a plan in mind to reconcile His relationship with His creation.

When Joseph went into Egypt ahead of Jacob, the Lord's ultimate goal was reconciliation of Joseph and his family. Moses was an instrument of the reconciliation between God and the children of Israel so that they could experience the land God promised to them. David and the prophets were agents of reconciliation between the Lord and Israel. Again and again and again, the Lord forgave the sins of His people.

The ultimate forgiveness, the ultimate opportunity for reconciliation, came through the gift of God's Son, Jesus, our Savior. Through Christ, God has forgiven us. Second Corinthians 5:18–19 puts it like this:

> *All this is from God, who reconciled us to himself through Christ and gave us the ministry of reconciliation: that God was reconciling the world to himself in Christ, not counting people's sins against them. And he has committed to us the message of reconciliation.*

How can we be reconciled with people who did us wrong? Forgiveness clears the path for a fresh start. It doesn't guarantee one, but it sets the stage. When the chain of unforgiveness is gone, there's room to reconcile through the power of the Holy Spirit.

Benefit 6: You open the door for restoration. A friendship, a marriage, a work relationship, a church, or a community can be restored after mutual acts of forgiveness. Consider Joseph. Not only was he reconciled with his father and his brothers, but the family relationship was also restored. They behaved like a family again.

Some of the benefits of forgiveness are inherent. If you forgive someone, you will experience freedom, but you will also grant freedom from hatred to your offender, whether or not that person knows or acknowledges it.

Other benefits of forgiveness are dependent upon circumstances. Reconciliation and restoration are two-way streets; they require the work of both parties. You may forgive someone but not be reconciled to him or her. You may be reconciled to someone without a full restoration of the relationship. Whether those two benefits of forgiveness occur or not, you have done what is right, and you will walk in freedom from the shackles of bitterness.

Christ came to set us free and to give us abundant life (Galatians 5:1; John 10:10). God doesn't want your life to be destroyed or for you to live in bondage. His plan for you is living a life full of His grace, peace, and love. Just as you didn't deserve to be hurt, neither do you deserve to live in bondage based on others' actions or inactions. Live in the freedom that God desires for you!

WORKBOOK

Chapter Three Questions

Question: We should glean wisdom from every unfortunate event in our lives. Do you know someone who is susceptible to a certain type of offense, such as repeated abuse or financial scams? How can we be truly forgiving while not falling for the same thing again?

_____

_____

_____

_____

_____

_____

_____

_____

_____

Question: Name some people from the Bible who exemplify forgiveness, aside from Joseph and Jesus. Read the accounts of both an Old Testament person and a New Testament person who forgave their offenders, such as David with King Saul, Stephen with those who martyred him, or Paul with those who persecuted him. What can you learn from each of them?

_____

_____

_____

_____

_____

_____

_____

_____

_____

_____

_____

Question: Imagine what a life of freedom would look like—freedom from bitterness, freedom from focus on your offender, potential freedom for the offender, and freedom for healing and possible restoration. Journal about how your life would be different if you fully experienced this freedom.

_____

_____

_____

_____

_____

_____

_____

_____

_____

_____

_____

Action: Look at the list of metaphors for unforgiveness (prison, poison, roadblock, play money, and cancer). Which one speaks most to you personally? Draw or find an image that illustrates this idea. Beside it, place an image that illustrates freedom. Caption your pictures with a verse about forgiveness.

Chapter Three Notes

_____

_____

_____

_____

_____

_____

_____

_____

_____

_____

_____

_____

_____

_____

_____

_____

_____

_____

_____

_____

_____

CHAPTER FOUR

The Unmerciful Servant

Children may not always recognize when they're supposed to be quiet, but sometimes that's exactly when they're most humorous. Take for example the following unplanned exchange during a sermon in church one week.

Pastor: "What must we do before we can receive God's forgiveness?"

Young Johnny: "Sin!"

Maybe young Johnny simply didn't know that the prior offense of sin is one we all have and will have again. None of us is without it, so none of us is without the need for forgiveness.

If you're going to walk in the freedom and healing that forgiveness brings, you'll need to remember that. At the foot of the cross, we all are broken and in need of the forgiveness of our Savior, Jesus Christ. We need forgiveness, and we need to forgive.

One passage in the Gospel of Matthew addresses both

sides of this forgiveness coin. Look first at Matthew 18: 21–22:

> *Then Peter came to Jesus and asked, "Lord, how many times shall I forgive my brother or sister who sins against me? Up to seven times?"*
>
> *Jesus answered, "I tell you, not seven times, but seventy-seven times."*

Some of us consider forgiving our brother seven times to be a bit stingy, and some of us think that it's being generous! But the point of Jesus' answer is that we are to be extravagant with our forgiveness. Jesus wasn't saying that we should forgive our brother literally or specifically 490 times. He was emphasizing the point that our forgiveness should be perpetual and continual. Forgiveness is part of who our Father is; therefore, it is to be part of our spiritual DNA as well.

Jesus went on in this passage to compare the kingdom of heaven to a king settling accounts with his servants:

> *Therefore, the kingdom of heaven is like a king who wanted to settle accounts with his servants. As he began the settlement, a man who owed him ten thousand bags of gold was brought to him. Since he was not able to pay, the master ordered that he and his wife and his children and all that he had be sold to repay the debt.*
>
> *At this the servant fell on his knees before him. "Be patient with me," he begged, "and I will pay back everything." The servant's master took pity on him, canceled the debt and let him go.*

But when that servant went out, he found one of his fellow servants who owed him a hundred silver coins. He grabbed him and began to choke him. "Pay back what you owe me!" he demanded.

His fellow servant fell to his knees and begged him, "Be patient with me, and I will pay it back."

But he refused. Instead, he went off and had the man thrown into prison until he could pay the debt. When the other servants saw what had happened, they were outraged and went and told their master everything that had happened.

Then the master called the servant in. "You wicked servant," he said, "I canceled all that debt of yours because you begged me to. Shouldn't you have had mercy on your fellow servant just as I had on you?" In anger his master handed him over to the jailers to be tortured, until he should pay back all he owed.

This is how my heavenly Father will treat each of you unless you forgive your brother or sister from your heart.
—Matthew 18:23–35

This servant owed his master ten thousand bags of gold! That would be millions of today's dollars, since gold fetches more than $1,400 per ounce at the time of this writing.[6] What did the servant ask for? Time. What did the master grant him? Full forgiveness of the debt. In exchange, the master expected his servant to be merciful to those around him as a sign of gratitude for the freedom he was given.

This is what our heavenly Father offers us: debt forgiveness, paid in full. In turn, He expects us to offer grace and forgiveness to others, as Jesus demonstrated in His prayer (Matthew 6:9–13). Forgiveness among Jesus' followers on earth should look like forgiveness in the kingdom of heaven.

Recognizing How Much We Have Been Forgiven

The master in Jesus' parable acted in mercy, as God acts in mercy toward us. The astronomical amount of money the servant owed is akin to the astronomical debt our sin has accrued for us. We are indebted to God by our sin and wickedness. When we're honest, we see how we have offended the Lord and hurt others.

There is a popular anecdote that the British theologian G.K. Chesterton once responded to a question in a London paper asking, "What is the primary problem of the world?" with the words: "I am the problem." It's not only others who need forgiveness; each of us is equally in need of it.

Until we recognize our need for forgiveness and the extent to which we have been pardoned, we will find it impossible to extend forgiveness to others. By the same token, we must never define ourselves or others exclusively by sin. If God can forgive us and show us mercy, we ought to be willing to do the same for other people. You might say, "Well, they don't deserve it!" And you might be right. But remember, you and I don't deserve God's forgiveness, either. If we did deserve forgiveness, it wouldn't be a gift; it wouldn't be grace.

Jesus came from heaven to the cross and gave Himself up sacrificially, paying the debt we owe and could never satisfy. Because of that, we can pour out mercy and forgiveness to others. The Lord uses us, as believers, to be conduits of His grace. But before we go handing out forgiveness without thought, we need to take the second step.

Naming Our Offenses and Our Offenders

Fourteenth-century philosopher William of Ockham posited that we must cut away from the equation that which is not immediately necessary in order to find the solution. In other words, we need to isolate the root issue.[7]

To forgive another person, we must isolate exactly what the offense is. A general statement such as "he did me wrong" won't work. Rather, be specific and precise about the exact offense requiring your forgiveness: "He belittled me and maligned my character in public and private."

We must also keep the offense confined. Don't talk to everybody but your offender. Don't take your issue to social media or the church parking lot or the family reunion. Follow Matthew 18:15–20, in which Jesus instructed His followers to go directly to the offending brother or sister and deal with the offense in person, if possible. When we approach the person we need to forgive, we need to keep in mind the third step toward forgiveness.

Don't Deny the Sin or Your Anger

Anger is like a "check engine" warning light in your car; it indicates that something is wrong and needs to be dealt with. Like with pain in the body, ignoring it won't make it go away. Ignoring or denying it will only make it worse. Anger will fester into bitterness and deeper anger, and it will infect all of your relationships, not just the one in which forgiveness is needed.

In the parable above, the master never pretended that the servant didn't owe him 10,000 bags of gold. He forgave the debt, but first he acknowledged it. When someone has sinned against you, acknowledge it. Don't deny it. Don't minimize it. Don't blow it out of proportion. Honestly recognize the offense, and then honestly recognize your hurt and anger.

Maybe you lost control because of what someone else said or did. Maybe you were rejected or betrayed. Maybe you have righteous indignation over injustice against someone else. Whatever the cause of your anger, be honest about it. Only then can you take the final step before offering forgiveness.

Accepting God's Direction

This last step to take before extending the hand of forgiveness is crucial. Forgiveness isn't easy. Forgiveness is, in fact, very difficult. It's supernatural. It's not something we can do on our own. Only the Holy Spirit can help us, especially when the offense is deep.

The Lord needs to be the only one to direct our steps in the journey of forgiveness. He says when and where and how. This isn't something we can rush, and it isn't something we can get around to whenever we want. It's a supernatural move accomplished in the power of the Holy Spirit.

Don't fret if it takes longer than some people think it

ought to take. Corrie ten Boom, who was arrested with her sister for hiding Jews in their home during World War II, knew the difficulty and reward of forgiveness.[8] Years after the war, she came face to face with one of the captors from the concentration camp where she had been held and where her sister had died, and he asked for her forgiveness.

Corrie ten Boom realized that forgiveness is not an emotion. She wrote of the experience that "forgiveness is an act of the will, and the will can function regardless of the temperature of the heart." Though she did not want to forgive her former guard, she followed God's command, and the emotions miraculously followed.

Every step toward the heart of God is a step toward peace and victory. Even if you wonder whether you can finish the journey of forgiveness, simply choose to start, trusting that He will help you at every junction.

Let's be like the master in the story in Matthew, pardoning even astronomical debt, as God has pardoned ours. Let's not be like the unmerciful servant, who was forgiven but refused to forgive.

Chapter Four Questions

Question: Have you ever needed to forgive the same person repeatedly? Did your forgiveness have a time limit or a point at which you decided that you would not forgive the person again? How is that different from the way in which God has and continues to forgive you?

_____

_____

_____

_____

_____

_____

_____

_____

_____

Question: What are some of the offenses for which God and others have forgiven you throughout your life? Do you see that forgiveness as deserved or merciful?

_____

_____

_____

_____

_____

_____

_____

_____

_____

_____

Journal: Take time to name your offenders and acknowledge their offenses against you. Be specific, honest, and objective. Then write down how their sins affected you, both how you were hurt by them and how you have responded emotionally to the hurt.

_____

_____

_____

_____

_____

_____

_____

_____

_____

_____

_____

Action: The Lord needs to be the one to direct your steps in the journey of forgiveness. Plan a special time to spend with the Lord this week in His Word and in prayer. Make use of such help as worship music, Bible study tools, and a prayer guide or journal. Reflect on and thank God for His astronomical forgiveness to you. Ask Him to guide you in how you can extend that forgiveness to those who have wronged you.

Chapter Four Notes

_____

_____

_____

_____

_____

_____

_____

_____

_____

_____

_____

_____

_____

_____

_____

_____

_____

_____

_____

_____

_____

_____

CHAPTER FIVE

Understanding Is Key

When they came to the place called the Skull, they crucified him there, along with the criminals—one on his right, the other on his left. Jesus said, "Father, forgive them, for they do not know what they are doing." And they divided up his clothes by casting lots.

The people stood watching, and the rulers even sneered at him. They said, "He saved others; let him save himself if he is God's Messiah, the Chosen One."

The soldiers also came up and mocked him. They offered him wine vinegar and said, "If you are the king of the Jews, save yourself."

There was a written notice above him, which read: THIS IS THE KING OF THE JEWS.

—Luke 23:33–38

Imagine this scene. The Jewish political and religious leaders came together to crucify Jesus. He endured supreme pain and merciless beatings before His crucifixion. Then He suffered yet more—the scorching heat, the crown of thorns, the blood, the bruises, the spikes in His hands and feet. The weight of His body pulled on the spikes as the cross was lifted and set in place.

In addition, Jesus faced immense spiritual opposition. He knew what it was to be betrayed, humiliated, abandoned, and overwhelmed. We can sense the cry of Jesus and feel the temptation to compromise. He felt the worst of man's brutality, yet even while He hung on the cross, He prayed to the Father to forgive those who were crucifying Him. Those around Him were taunting and mocking Him, expressing contempt, but still He said, "Father, forgive them" (Luke 23:34). If we follow in Jesus' footsteps, we know that He will provide all that is needed for us to offer that same grace.

This is one of the most shocking yet wonderful episodes in human history. It's shocking because the creation was murdering the Creator, and it's wonderful because, at the same time, the Creator was saving the creation. He looked past His personal agony and saw man's need. It wasn't easy, but He looked beyond the fault and recognized the desperate need.

What would it look like if you and I, who are followers of Jesus, would reach beyond our feelings to somebody else's need? It would look like real forgiveness.

If we're going to give God glory, we must express who He is in our lives. We need to look beyond our parents' shortcomings and the deficiencies in our siblings, friends, and co-workers in order to give them what they desperately need. We need to seek an understanding.

There are all kinds of influences affecting people's behavior. Sometimes we only look at the surface, but there's a story behind every act. We need to learn to look for what

God wills us to see.

Isaiah 53:12 prophesied that the Savior, the Messiah, would pray for the transgressors. Christ mediates between holy God and sinful man. He died so that it would be justifiably possible for God to cancel out the debt we owed; otherwise, we would be eternally lost.

Don't look at the situation. Instead, look to "Jesus, the pioneer and perfecter of faith" (Hebrews 12:2). Your situations and experiences are all to glorify God. When the world attacks and you retaliate, the world is not surprised. After all, that's what we're supposed to do when we're wronged, according to human nature. On the other hand, when you respond in grace and mercy, it shocks the world. People will wonder why, and you will be able to answer that you forgive because your God forgives.

Grace Through Understanding

The grace we need in order to forgive is born out of understanding. In the last chapter, we touched on the fact that we must rely on the Holy Spirit and trust God's direction on the journey to forgiveness. Understanding, as given by the Holy Spirit, is absolutely crucial to our ability to forgive.

We must understand that the power to forgive only comes from the Holy Spirit. We are out of our minds if we think that we can be like Jesus and pull this off on our own! God has given us access to all that we need to do what He told us to do. He never commands us to do something without giving us what's essential to accomplish it.

First Corinthians 2:10 says, "...these are the things

God has revealed to us by his Spirit. The Spirit searches all things, even the deep things of God." Verse 16 says, "We have the mind of Christ." Paul urged the Philippians, "Let this mind be in you, which was also in Christ Jesus" (Philippians 2:5 KJV). Paul said "let" because we can hinder the mind of Christ from ruling and reigning in us by refusing to receive His Word and do what He says.

We will never have a truly deep understanding of our and the offender's issues without the Holy Spirit. When we allow the Holy Spirit to give us the mind of Christ and help us forgive, we can arrive at an understanding and be gracious enough to give the gift of forgiveness. Any other form of forgiveness will fall short.

We must acknowledge that understanding is crucial. Forgiveness isn't head knowledge. It isn't saying the right words. It isn't looking the other way without addressing the offense, the offender, and your feelings. There's no magic wand to wave here. Forgiveness requires the hard work of thinking in order to understand. We have to pursue knowledge and insight in the power of the Spirit.

Remember, the enemy thrives on lies, distortions of the truth, misunderstandings, and cloudy thinking. He is "the father of lies" (John 8:44).

We have to ask questions, such as:

"Why would she say such a thing about me?"

"Why does it bother me so much when he does that?"

"Is this in keeping with that person's character that I've experienced?"

Always remember that the enemy is a master deceiver. When we know that there's a plan of deception behind the scenes, we can approach the situation with a clearer perspective.

Finally, we must understand the other person through the Spirit. This is possibly the hardest element of understanding, but it's indispensable. We should understand that few people actually mean to hurt us deeply. People wound us because of their experiences. When we come to understand that they didn't mean to hurt us as badly as we're hurting, it helps us to overcome the emotions and choose to forgive.

Jesus was able to forgive those who were crucifying Him because He knew that they were operating from a limited understanding and had fallen prey to the enemy's careful plan of deception. Perhaps you've heard the saying "hurt people hurt people." It's true. It's also true that deceived people deceive people.

If we understand somebody else's plight, it makes all the difference in how we approach him or her. We need to consider a person's past. We may not know the backstory, but we need to understand that personal issues and brokenness affect behavior and can make people insecure, passive, pessimistic, critical, insensitive, or suspicious. Some hurt people seek approval by whatever means it takes. It may seem like they're running for a popularity contest, but in many instances, they have been rejected or neglected.

Trying to understand where the offender is coming from helps us to have compassion and makes it a bit easier to forgive. It reminds us that if not for the grace of God, we would look just like our offenders. We were all delivered from something and fall short of God's perfect standard. If He delivered you and me, He can deliver others.

Compassion is a vital ingredient in our understanding of our offenders. Matthew 9:36 says, "When he [Jesus] saw the crowds, he had compassion on them, because they were harassed and helpless, like sheep without a shepherd." Compassion allows us to peer through the window of other people's souls and glimpse their struggles in order to understand the story behind their behavior. Take a look in the mirror and think of how compassionate God has been to you. Surely you should exemplify the One you claim to follow.

Compassion begins with internal transformation—a heart change—and then moves to external manifestation. That's how you can willingly give the gift of forgiveness to an offender who doesn't deserve it. Compassion breeds insight. Insight breeds empathy. Empathy makes room for forgiveness.

Three Conventional Responses

Traditionally, there are three responses human beings have to getting hurt.

Tribalism

Like the feuding Hatfield and McCoy families in the late nineteenth century, groups of people who have experienced offenses may resort to tribalism, which can result in escalating tensions and incitement to violence. The offended party corners others to tell them what's happened and tries to win support. Whole families, communities, or nations may come together to harbor a grudge and possibly exact vengeance. We learn it on the playground in elementary school; we just become more sophisticated with it as we age.

Tribalism is why families don't get along. Grandma was upset because great auntie took Grandma's roast pan and never brought it back. Two generations later, the two sides still aren't speaking. Go to Walmart and get another roast pan! It's better to move on!

"Eye for an Eye" Justice

We may like to quote "eye for eye, tooth for tooth" (Exodus 21:24) to justify retaliation. This was not a biblical mandate to even the score. It was a directive to eliminate tribalism and seek reasonable justice. It was a rule for enforcing proportional punishment. Otherwise, there could have been continually escalating war between the two parties.

We need to remember Jesus' words regarding retribution in the Sermon on the Mount:

> You have heard that it was said, "Eye for eye, and tooth for tooth." But I tell you, do not resist an evil person. If anyone slaps you on the right cheek, turn to them the other cheek also. And if anyone wants to sue you and take your shirt, hand over your coat as well. If anyone forces you to go one mile, go with them two miles. Give to the one who asks you, and do not turn away from the one who wants to borrow from you.
> —*Matthew 5:38–42*

Jesus did not support retaliation. He showed us another way—the way of humility, generosity, and forgiveness.

Forgiveness

Forgiveness is more beneficial than retaliation because it doesn't look for justice by evening the score. To be fair, forgiveness doesn't eliminate the natural and logical consequences of violating the law. Instead, forgiveness looks to pursue peace. It looks beyond the issue and does not define the offender exclusively by the offense. Forgiveness opens the door to reconciliation and restoration.

God wills that we live in His peace. He desires that we know His joy through personal communion with Him. Don't settle for less. He wills for you to be abundantly blessed. Life happens to all of us; we all have ebbs and flows. But life is far too short to be weighed down with yesterday's issues. Gain wisdom through each experience, but don't let anything stifle your progress in Christ.

Following in His Steps

Imagine walking into a prison cell that holds your offender, who is tied to a chair and unable to move. Imagine picking up a bat. You're poised and ready to strike. Then you pause for a moment and think, "A Christian is supposed to forgive, so I will choose to forgive because I'm a Christian."

You verbalize your forgiveness to your offender, but your anger is still simmering. You haven't addressed the offense or your feelings, and you don't have any understanding of why the offense was committed. Your words of forgiveness are premature and artificial, and they won't take healthy root.

Let me give you another scenario. Instead of forgiving superficially, you decide to take the bat and beat your offender, hard, because the Bible says to take an eye for an eye. Now you've allowed yourself to justify your anger, and you've released your bitterness and hatred on your offender. The problem is that the release passed quickly and wasn't as gratifying as you had hoped. That is how unforgiveness and bitterness work. They put you on a destructive path, not a path toward healing.

Consider this final option: you allow yourself to feel the pain you felt when this person mistreated you, but instead of retaliating or quickly giving a false forgiveness, you decide to do nothing but weigh your pain. Then you sense Jesus walking into the room and standing next to you. He impresses a thought on your heart. What is it? What would He say to you if your offender were tied down and you were holding a weapon for revenge?

We know how He responded when He was on the cross. We know how He reinstated Peter after Peter's bald-faced denial of Jesus the night He was betrayed. We know how God treated the Israelites when they repented—again and again and again and again.

Will we, in the power of the indwelling Holy Spirit, follow in the steps of our Lord and Savior, Jesus Christ, who honestly, freely, and perfectly forgave? If He could, we can.

Chapter Five Questions

Question: What would it be like if you, as a follower of Christ, were to look beyond your feelings to somebody else's desperate need? Consider your offenders. What are their greatest needs? Are they even aware of these needs? What hurts, problems, or misunderstandings in their lives may have contributed to their offenses?

_____

_____

_____

_____

_____

_____

_____

_____

_____

Question: Describe a time when you unintentionally hurt another person because of ignorance, selfishness, or personal hurts. What sort of response would have helped you to acknowledge your offense, yet receive God's grace and learn from your mistakes?

_____

_____

_____

_____

_____

_____

_____

_____

_____

_____

_____

_____

Journal: Write out a prayer to the Lord, asking His Spirit to guide you in understanding your offender's needs, in understanding the nature of forgiveness, and in understanding His power to help you forgive.

_____

_____

_____

_____

_____

_____

_____

_____

_____

_____

_____

_____

Action: Read a book or listen to a testimony about a Christian who was forgiven of a prodigal past before coming to Christ, or one who caused problems within the church even after being saved. What contributed to this person's bad choices and sins? How did this person hurt others, either intentionally or unintentionally? How did he or she experience forgiveness? How does trying to see the world from your offender's perspective help in understanding his or her needs, hurts, and sins?

Chapter Five Notes

CHAPTER SIX

Seeking Restoration
and Reconciliation

If you were to summarize the fifteenth chapter of the Gospel of Luke, you could entitle it: "A lost coin, a lost sheep, and a lost son."

Jesus began by talking about a lost sheep and a lost coin. He used these stories to demonstrate how the Pharisees should have acted when a lost sinner was found. When He got to the longer story of the lost son, He revealed how the Pharisees actually behaved.

Jesus' story of the prodigal son can teach us about forgiveness, as well:

Jesus continued: "There was a man who had two sons. The younger one said to his father, 'Father, give me my share of the estate.' So he divided his property between them.

"Not long after that, the younger son got together all he had, set off for a distant country and there squandered his wealth in wild living. After he had spent everything, there was a severe famine in that whole country, and he began

to be in need. So he went and hired himself out to a citizen of that country, who sent him to his fields to feed pigs. He longed to fill his stomach with the pods that the pigs were eating, but no one gave him anything.

"When he came to his senses, he said, 'How many of my father's hired servants have food to spare, and here I am starving to death! I will set out and go back to my father and say to him: Father, I have sinned against heaven and against you. I am no longer worthy to be called your son; make me like one of your hired servants.' So he got up and went to his father.

"But while he was still a long way off, his father saw him and was filled with compassion for him; he ran to his son, threw his arms around him and kissed him.

"The son said to him, 'Father, I have sinned against heaven and against you. I am no longer worthy to be called your son.'

"But the father said to his servants, 'Quick! Bring the best robe and put it on him. Put a ring on his finger and sandals on his feet. Bring the fattened calf and kill it. Let's have a feast and celebrate. For this son of mine was dead and is alive again; he was lost and is found.' So they began to celebrate.

"Meanwhile, the older son was in the field. When he came near the house, he heard music and dancing. So he called one of the servants and asked him what was going on. 'Your brother has come,' he replied, 'and your father has killed the fattened calf because he has him back safe and sound.'

"The older brother became angry and refused to go in. So his father went out and pleaded with him. But he answered his father, 'Look! All these years I've been slaving for you and never disobeyed your orders. Yet you never gave me even a young goat so I could celebrate with my friends. But when this son of yours who has squandered your property with prostitutes comes home, you kill the fattened calf for him!'

"'My son,' the father said, 'you are always with me, and everything I have is yours. But we had to celebrate and be
glad, because this brother of yours was dead and is alive
again; he was lost and is found.'"

—*Luke 15:11-32*

In this story, Jesus captured three personalities. First
was the father, a picture of a loving, gracious, and forgiving God. The father waited for his son to return. He even
rushed to meet him, perhaps to protect him from unnecessary criticism he may have received from others because
of the disgrace he had brought to the family. This father
didn't look at blunders and mishaps. He loved his son
simply and genuinely.

The elder son was a picture of the Pharisees. To be fair,
he had good points as well as bad. He was obedient, hard-
working, and morally straight. On the other hand, he was
proud, haughty, and high-minded, and he had no fellow-
ship with his father. He focused on his brother's sin as
opposed to his brother's repentance. Instead of welcoming
and celebrating his younger brother, he chose to harbor ill
feelings.

Last was the younger son, the offender in this story. He
did things that were wrong and contrary to Jewish tradition and the customs of Jewish families. His rebellion
resulted in immoral living. He hit rock bottom before re-
alizing his need to repent and return. His conduct was
willful and inexcusable, yet the forgiveness he received
was absolute.

This prodigal son serves as a picture of many of us. He
represents every person today who stands in need of the
Savior. He searched abroad for everything that was

already at home. All of the abundance, freedom, and joy we seek is waiting for us in the arms of our heavenly Father.

In the Jewish tradition, the father reserved the right, upon his death, to bestow two-thirds of his estate on his eldest son and one-third on the younger, but he could divide his property during his lifetime if he wished. In the case of this parable, the father agreed to give the younger son one-third of his estate. The son said, "Give me," not "may I" or "please." He asked for both his inheritance and his independence. The father gave him both.

The son had no concern about hurting his father or damaging the estate. He took the resources and went away to live his own life. Maybe he thought that his father asked too much of him. *Prodigal* means one who lives lavishly and spends money extravagantly.[9] The younger son spent his inheritance on wild living, drunkenness, and immorality. He had not worked for the money or earned it, and he didn't appreciate what he was given.

Then the famine struck. Any time you have it all, making friends based on living up to their social class and standard of living, and then lose your resources, you will suddenly be the loneliest person in the world. A famine came, and all of his supposed friends were nowhere to be seen. He was alone and destitute in the midst of a widespread crisis.

He was starving. He thought that the world would satisfy, nourish, and provide for him, but instead he found himself enslaved and humiliated. He never thought that he, a fine Jew who previously wouldn't even have considered being connected with a Gentile, would be working with hogs in a foreign land. A Jew wouldn't touch pork, so for him to be tending pigs and eating their food meant that he was desperate. He was broken, and there was no one there to understand.

Luke 15:17 tells us that the younger son eventually "came to his senses." Before that, he had been out of his mind, not in touch with reality or consistent with who he was. He realized that his father could provide for him and save him from starvation, so he made a plan to return home. He said, "I will set out and go back to my father" (Luke 15:18). Repentance needs to be more than just a thought; it requires action.

He went home, which led to the famous scene of his father meeting him, rejoicing, and throwing a party to celebrate his return. Then we see the equally instructive reaction of the jealous and resentful older brother. The father forgave, and the older brother did not. What can we learn about forgiveness from each of their responses?

The Barrier Attitudes

It's critical to evaluate the attitudes that block forgiveness and reconciliation. The first of those barrier attitudes is an unwillingness to admit that we ourselves need forgiveness and grace. Likely, the older brother thought that he was fully in the right. He didn't consider the things he had said and done that required his father's forgiveness, or maybe he thought that his offenses paled in comparison to his brother's.

If we expect to be able to forgive one another, we have to be aware of our need for forgiveness and remember how much we have been forgiven. When we focus on the sin instead of the repentance, we tend to become "history majors," harping on the offense even when the offender is standing there, hat in hand, seeking reconciliation. It's inevitable that we will have a hard time forgiving if we focus on the offense as the older brother did.

The second barrier attitude is a refusal to pursue understanding. Failing to try to understand the offender and yourself can be a hindrance to forgiveness. Consider your offender's perspective and take a look at his or her background and character. Reflect on the offense and try to understand it from every angle. Don't block forgiveness, but be fair to yourself and your pain. Forgiveness is not the denial of true pain.

A third hindrance to forgiveness is talking instead of praying. It's okay to ask others for guidance when you've been hurt, but remember to turn to God for the ultimate wisdom. Some people can feed into the foolishness and cause an issue to go from a spark to a blaze, producing even more anger and bitterness. Not everyone has your best interest at heart, but God does. Get on your knees and pray, and you'll be surprised how much He can soften your heart and clear your mind.

The Difference Between Reconciliation and Restoration

Both restoration and reconciliation are two-way streets. Some people choose to hold on to ill feelings, mistakenly reasoning that if they forgive, then their offenders will win. However, you can be reconciled without necessarily being restored. Reconciliation is a mutual truce, a peace treaty of sorts. You may have a level of reconnection, but not necessarily a deep or intimate reunion. It's still a good place to be, because it allows you to move on with your life.

Restoration is a mutual agreement to rebuild the relationship. Reconciliation may end with you going your separate ways, while restoration is healing the relationship and choosing to continue on together.

Recognizing When Restoration Is Not Possible or Wise

If the person who offended you is deceased or if a former spouse has remarried, you can't restore the relationship back to how it used to be. If the relationship was unstable, destructive, dangerous, or volatile, it's unwise to restore the relationship. You need to forgive an abuser—in God's time and way—but you do not need to pursue reconciliation, unless the Lord miraculously opens that door.

In such situations, forgiveness doesn't lead to reconciliation and restoration on a human level, but God offers us peace about the person and the offense. Ultimately, we should not look for the kind of peace the world offers, but rather the peace of God. Jesus said, "Peace I leave with you; my peace I give you. I do not give to you as the world gives. Do not let your hearts be troubled and do not be afraid" (John 14:27). God's peace will keep and preserve you in this life.

The prodigal son came back home. He longed for the

father's peace. When he returned, his father showed him a heart of mercy. Where others saw a mess, his father saw a beloved son.

The father told his servants, "Quick! Bring the best robe and put it on him. Put a ring on his finger and sandals on his feet" (Luke 15:22). The robe signifies righteousness, and the ring symbolizes authority to represent the Father and the Kingdom. If God can forgive and restore that son, then He can do the same for you and me.

Maybe you can identify, in some measure, with the prodigal son. Maybe you have forsaken your relationship with God and lived in rebellion. No matter how far you have gone, God loves you and wants you to come back home.

Maybe you can identify with the older brother, resentful that your brother's offenses seem to be forgiven so easily. Remember that all forgiveness comes at a cost, and that cost was the blood of Jesus on a cross. The forgiveness Jesus bought is offered to all, bitter brother and prodigal son.

Remove the barriers in your heart and allow yourself to forgive. Pursue reconciliation and restoration whenever possible. Forgiveness is a process, and you may never reach the final destination of restoration. Even so, forgiving those who hurt you will give you personal freedom. Choose to live in the liberty God offers you.

WORKBOOK

Chapter Six Questions

Question: With which character in the story of the prodigal son do you most identify—the forgiving father, the self-righteous and angry older brother, or the selfish and, eventually, repentant younger brother? Why? How can you become less like one of the sons and more like the father?

_____

_____

_____

_____

_____

_____

_____

_____

_____

Question: How should you respond when the offender isn't repentant, does not acknowledge actions as hurtful or wrong, or continues to engage in hurtful behavior? What might forgiveness look like in such a situation, and how would it differ if the offender were truly repentant?

_____

_____

_____

_____

_____

_____

_____

_____

_____

_____

_____

_____

Journal: Look at the list you made in Chapter One of relationships that need forgiveness. Journal about your ultimate goal for each of these. In which relationships may reconciliation be possible and something that you can safely pursue? In which relationships is full restoration a possibility? In which situations can the relationship not be restored, and how can you protect yourself and others from further hurt while continuing to forgive?

_____

_____

_____

_____

_____

_____

_____

_____

_____

_____

_____

_____

Action: What are some helpful guidelines for knowing when, how, and to whom to talk about an interpersonal conflict? How can you seek wisdom and spiritual counsel without spreading the bitterness that comes from getting other people to take up an offense for you? Make out a bullet-point list of Scripture-based guidelines and commit to talking to the right people in the right way.

Chapter Six Notes

CHAPTER SEVEN

Living in God's Peace

We've already looked some at the story of Joseph in the second half of the book of Genesis. Recall that when Joseph's brothers arrived in Egypt, seeking relief from the famine in Canaan, they unknowingly encountered the brother they'd sold into slavery so many years ago—only now Joseph was second-in-command to Pharaoh himself, a position of extraordinary power. He could exact any and all revenge he wanted over those diabolical brothers.

Rather than lord his power over them, however, Joseph chose to forgive his brothers, much to their relief and amazement. Then their father, Jacob, and all of Joseph's family moved to Egypt to the best land available and were warmly welcomed by Pharaoh. In due time, Jacob died, and suddenly the brothers were worried again. Had Joseph been biding his time, being kind to them for the sake of his father? Would this be the day that he exacted his revenge?

> *When Joseph's brothers saw that their father was dead,*
> *they said, "What if Joseph holds a grudge against us and*
> *pays us back for all the wrongs we did to him?" So they sent*
> *word to Joseph, saying, "Your father left these instructions*
> *before he died: 'This is what you are to say to Joseph: I ask*
> *you to forgive your brothers the sins and the wrongs they*
> *committed in treating you so badly.' Now please forgive*
> *the sins of the servants of the God of your father." When*
> *their message came to him, Joseph wept.*
>
> *His brothers then came and threw themselves down before*
> *him. "We are your slaves," they said.*
>
> *But Joseph said to them, "Don't be afraid. Am I in the place*
> *of God? You intended to harm me, but God intended it for*
> *good to accomplish what is now being done, the saving of*
> *many lives. So then, don't be afraid. I will provide for you*
> *and your children." And he reassured them and spoke*
> *kindly to them.*
>
> **—Genesis 50:15–21**

If you ever need an example of how forgiveness leads to living in peace, this is it. Joseph forgave his brothers, and the whole family was not only saved, but also restored to peaceful relations. Doesn't that sound more appealing than revenge?

The Transformative Power of Forgiveness

Revenge will give you a temporary, false high. Forgiveness will offer you lasting, true peace. Even if there isn't full reconciliation or restoration, you can walk free of the bonds of bitterness and unforgiveness. Jesus came, died, and rose again to offer us that kind of liberty. Receive it.

As I've mentioned before, this isn't human nature. It's

a supernatural gift that we first have to receive from God. Then we must rely on the Holy Spirit to help us through the process of extending forgiveness to others.

Romans 12:2 tells us, "Do not conform to the pattern of this world, but be transformed by the renewing of your mind." The word for *transformed* comes from the same Greek root as our English word *metamorphosis*.[10] Going through transformation involves renewing our minds so that we have the mind of Christ (Philippians 2:5). Transformation reaches deeper than conformity; it reaches far within our inward nature to bring about a fundamental change. This transformation includes forgiveness, and when we practice forgiveness, we live in God's peace.

While the Old Testament gives us a story of forgiveness that leads to peace, the New Testament provides extra teaching on the subject:

> *Do not repay anyone evil for evil. Be careful to do what is right in the eyes of everyone. If it is possible, as far as it depends on you, live at peace with everyone. Do not take revenge, my dear friends, but leave room for God's wrath, for it is written: "It is mine to avenge; I will repay," says the Lord. On the contrary: "If your enemy is hungry, feed him; if he is thirsty, give him something to drink. In doing this, you will heap burning coals on his head." Do not be overcome by evil, but overcome evil with good.*
> **—Romans 12:17–21**

Live above reproach. How many situations in life would be resolved if we were to live at peace with everyone and "overcome evil with good" (Romans 12:21). Instead of getting mad, smashing dishes, and kicking the dog, we could go off quietly with a root beer and come back later when we had calmed down. God never intended for us to think with our emotions.

Sometimes you just have to walk away so that you can eventually have an honorable and noble response, because one way or another, our responses to difficult situations are visible to the people around us. You will give God glory and be a testimony if you respond to offense in a manner that's inconsistent with the world but parallel to the Word of God. The world will come to you to know more about this Savior who keeps you sane.

This doesn't mean that you won't clench your fist or cry in the bathroom, but you must trust God's Spirit in you to keep you from doing what you really want to do. In the journey to forgiving someone else, think carefully and act with discretion and deliberation, relying on the Spirit to guide and empower your responses.

A Life Above Reproach

James wrote, "My dear brothers and sisters, take note of this: Everyone should be quick to listen, slow to speak and slow to become angry, because human anger does not produce the righteousness that God desires" (James 1:19–20). Thinking before you act and living above reproach will go a long way toward helping you live in peace with all. We are commanded to live peaceably with others if at all possible. Now, it's true that some people have no interest in living in peace. They are grumblers and complainers, fighters, power builders, and warmongers—and sometimes they come to church!

The implication in the scripture is that it's not always possible, but "as much as lieth in you," you should "live peaceably with all men" (Romans 12:18 KJV). God has made it possible, through the Holy Spirit, for us to pursue peace. Listen to the wisdom of the Holy Spirit, while also being careful when people want to talk to you about other people and situations that upset them. We should labor to have peace and harmony.

We walk around in defeat when we harbor anger, malice, and unforgiveness in our hearts. God wants us to have freedom. That's why He wants us to forgive and know His peace regardless of what's going on around us. I can't control what another person does, says, or thinks, but I can control what I do, say, and think. Don't ever throw in the towel and give up on doing what's right. Bring God glory with your words, actions, and thoughts.

Conflict should never be introduced by the believer. We should be the ones bringing about peace. However, peace doesn't come at the sacrifice of truth, such as ignoring injustice just to get along. If it's wrong, we call it wrong.

What determines whether we should defend ourselves or turn the other cheek? Jesus alone. We need to follow His instructions in every specific circumstance. Sometimes He will tell us to be silent; sometimes He will tell us to speak. He alone is the Prince of Peace, and we're to follow His directions as written in the Bible as we live out His mission of peace.

Learning When to Sacrifice Your "Rights"

To live in God's peace, we must refrain from revenge, and that is not easy. God tells us to do something that goes against the grain of our human nature. We don't naturally extend forgiveness to those who have wronged us. We want to fight and right the wrong, not forgive, but God commands us, "Recompense to no man evil for evil" (Romans 12:17 KJV). Note, He didn't say that evil wouldn't be done to us. He didn't say that we would not be wronged and treated unjustly.

Instead of taking matters into our own hands, we should leave space for divine retribution, "for it is written, Vengeance is mine; I will repay, saith the Lord" (Romans 12:19 KJV). God knows how to take care of us. Any time we respond with vengeance, we give victory to evil. Vengeance belongs to the Lord.

We would have a wonderful place to live if the world abided by this rule, but it isn't the way the world operates. This text, however, was written to believers. Vengeance belongs to God; it's not your possession. If you use it, you're taking something from God that you have no right to take, like someone stealing your car and trashing it. It might look like your enemy is getting away with everything, but God says that He will repay. God's wrath is a fearsome thing, and we should pray for those who are headed in its direction.

Romans 12:20 tells us that if we feed our enemies and give them something to drink, we "will heap burning coals" on their heads. The King James Version uses the term "coals of fire," which is a reference to an Egyptian ritual. When a man was repentant and wanted to convert, he would take a pan of hot coals and lay it on his head as a symbol.[11] Sometimes leaving people to themselves is all it takes for God to speak to them. The more they repress their guilt and ignore it, the more wrath they store up for the day of judgment. God will avenge you. You just need to walk in His peace.

Although the other party may deserve retribution, we should not do wrong in order to even the score. It is just as wrong no matter who does it! Revenge can never bring God glory. We will never even the score; we'll just go back and forth in a vicious cycle. At work, at school, in our very homes, we need to be careful. Many of us live together as families, but can't stand one another! What a tragedy to miss out on God's peace and joy in our lives.

The peace of God is an inner condition that can endure even the stormiest of times. This extraordinary peace goes beyond all understanding; it is above human comprehension (Philippians 4:7). You will be overwhelmed when you take matters into your own hands, but when you give your pain, burdens, and worries to the Lord, He will give you perfect peace.

Every step you take along this journey of forgiveness is a demonstration of your dependence upon God. Let His peace reign in your heart, rule in your mind, and have precedence in your life.

WORKBOOK

Chapter Seven Questions

Question: What is your initial, natural response when someone wrongs you? How can you give in less and less to your natural response and let the Holy Spirit guide and empower you for a supernatural response?

_____

_____

_____

_____

_____

_____

_____

_____

_____

Question: Describe a time when the Lord led you to keep silent on a matter, as well as a time when He led you to speak up for truth in a particular situation. When you are led to speak up and take an unpopular (but biblical) stand on an issue, how can you do so without creating unnecessary conflict?

_____

_____

_____

_____

_____

_____

_____

_____

_____

_____

Journal: Describe a time when you planned to take revenge against someone who hurt you. If your efforts for revenge were accomplished, did you feel better afterwards? How did you disrupt God's better justice, as well as thwart His plans for you? If you have been scheming and dreaming about revenge, surrender your plans to God and commit to letting Him enact justice in His time and way.

_____

_____

_____

_____

_____

_____

_____

_____

_____

_____

_____

Action: What are some ways you can live as a peace-maker in the midst of the conflicts in your life? Even if reconciliation and restoration are not possible, what steps can you take to promote peace, both inward and outward? How can your choice to live in God's peace in the midst of a difficult situation help draw others to Christ?

Chapter Seven Notes

_____

_____

_____

_____

_____

_____

_____

_____

_____

_____

_____

_____

_____

_____

_____

_____

_____

_____

_____

_____

_____

_____

CONCLUSION

Change the Ending of the Story

Life is an intersection of stories: mine plus yours, his family's plus her family's, this community plus that city, this nation and that nation. Other people have contributed—for good or for ill—to your story, and vice versa. You've changed some trajectories in your own life and in others' lives. Until a person goes home to be with the Lord, the story isn't over.

You can continue on the dark path of bitterness and resentment, regularly rehashing past hurts and wounds, until you can hardly see the path you're walking—or you can change the ending. You can choose to forgive and set yourself free to walk a path filled with light. Forgiveness marks turning points to good endings.

You will be wounded by others, and you get to choose your response. Will you nurse that hurt? Will it follow you to bed, to work, and into current and future relationships? Will it influence your decisions in negative ways? Or will you learn from it, then forgive, so that you can be both wiser and free?

Choose Freedom!

There is an enemy who stokes division and discord. There are hurt people who hurt people. We hurt each other. It's all part and parcel of living in this fallen world. There's just no getting around this reality.

Forgiveness is hard. We can offer genuine forgiveness only through the leading of God and the power of the Holy Spirit. We're tempted to shirk this difficult calling. Unforgiveness seems easier, but it casts shadows on our lives and our relationships.

We're not doomed to live lives constricted by division, discord, hurt, bitterness, and resentment. Christ showed us a better way, a way of freedom. Seek understanding. Pursue compassion. Follow the Lord's leading on the journey toward forgiveness and reap the benefits.

When we choose true forgiveness, not its imposters, we experience the freedom that Jesus died to bring us. It changes the ending of your story, and it can change the ending of someone else's as well. What a glorious gift! Choose to live in the freedom God wants for you. Change your story!

About the Author

Pastor Larry J. Mouton Jr. is a native of New Iberia, Louisiana. He is married to Reba Mouton, and they are the parents of two children, Hanna and Joshuah. Pastor Mouton is licensed and ordained and has been in ministry nearly two decades. He holds a bachelor's in theology and a master's in Christian education from Southwestern Baptist Theological Seminary in Fort Worth, Texas. He serves as the pastor of No Greater Love Baptist Church in Tampa, Florida. You can connect with Pastor Larry at: www.larrymoutonjr.com.

REFERENCES

Notes

[1] Hemingway, Ernest. "The Horns of the Bull: A Short Story." June 1, 1936. Esquire Publishing Company, 1936.

[2] King Jr., Martin Luther. Quoted in Michael Sullivan, "The Forgotten Speech by Martin Luther King Jr.: King Was More Than a Civil Rights Leader," The Odyssey Online, March 1, 2016. https://www.theodysseyonline.com/loving-your-enemies-the-forgotten-speech-by-martin-luther-king-jr.

[3] ten Boom, Corrie. "Guidepost Classics: Corrie ten Boom on Forgiveness." Guideposts. July 24, 2014. https://www.guideposts.org/better-living/positive-living/guideposts-classics-corrie-ten-boom-on-forgiveness.

[4] Lamott, Anne. *Traveling Mercies: Some Thoughts on Faith.* Knopf Doubleday, 2000.

[5] Buechner, Frederick. *Wishful Thinking: A Theological ABC.* Harper & Row, 1973.

[6] "Gold Price Today." Kitco. August 26, 2019.

https://www.kitco.com/gold-price-today-usa/.

[7] Spade, Paul Vincent and Claude Panaccio. "William of Ockham." In *The Stanford Encyclopedia of Philosophy*, Spring 2019 ed., edited by Edward N. Zalta. https://plato.stanford.edu/archives/spr2019/entries/ockham/.

[8] ten Boom, "Guideposts Classics: Corrie ten Boom on Forgiveness."

[9] "Prodigal." Lexico. https://www.lexico.com/en/definition/prodigal.

[10] Souter, Alexander. "μεταμορφόω." In *Pocket Lexicon to the Greek New Testament*. Oxford University Press, 1917.

[11] Klassen, William. "Coals of Fire: Sign of Repentance or Revenge? (Rom. 12:20; Prov. 25:22)." In *New Testament Studies*, vol. 9 (1963), p. 343.

Made in the USA
Columbia, SC
28 July 2020